Janice VanCleave's Wild, Wacky, and Weird Science Experiments

Janice VanCleave's Wild, Wacky, and Weird Biology Experiments

ROSEN PUBLISHING

New York

This edition published in 2017 by:
The Rosen Publishing Group, Inc.
29 East 21st Street
New York, NY 10010

Library of Congress Cataloging-in-Publication Data

Names: VanCleave, Janice Pratt, author..
Title: Janice Vancleave's wild, wacky, and weird biology experiments / Janice VanCleave.
Other titles: Wild, wacky, and weird biology experiments
Description: New York : Rosen Central, 2017. | Series: Janice Vancleave's wild, wacky, and weird science experiments | Includes bibliographical references and index.
Identifiers: LCCN 2016008910| ISBN 9781477789674 (library bound) | ISBN 9781477789650 (pbk.) | ISBN 9781477789667 (6-pack)
Subjects: LCSH: Biology--Experiments--Juvenile literature.
Classification: LCC QH316.5 .V364 2016 | DDC 570.78--dc23
LC record available at http://lccn.loc.gov/2016008910

Manufactured in China

CONTENTS

INTRODUCTION

Biology is the study of the way living organisms behave and interact. Earth has been supporting the tiniest of single-celled living things for as many as 3.5 billion years. Arthropods, fish, plants, and mammals followed. Humans evolved about 200,000 years ago. The mysterious, ever-changing nature of living organisms makes it a popular branch of science to study.

The people who choose biology as a career do a variety of work. Field biologists may work outdoors in remote ecosystems. Other scientists work in laboratories and study topics as varied as cures for diseases, new marine species, or human DNA. Zoologists study animals and botanists study plants. Most study life on Earth, but astrobiologists search for life outside our planet. All these people have something in common: They are constantly asking questions to learn even more about living things.

This book is a collection of science experiments about biology. How does a layer of fat keep an animal warm? Why do hummingbirds have long, slender bills? How do soil nutrients reach a plant's leaves? You will find the answers to these and many other questions by doing the experiments in this book.

HOW TO USE THIS BOOK

Before you get started, be sure to read each experiment completely before beginning. The following sections are included for all the experiments.

» **PURPOSE:** *The basic goals for the experiment.*

» **MATERIALS:** ***A list of supplies you will need.***

You will experience less frustration and more fun if you gather all the necessary materials for the experiments before you begin. You lose your train of thought when you have to shop and search for supplies.

» **PROCEDURE:** ***Step-by-step instructions on how to perform the experiment.***

Follow each step very carefully, never skip steps, and do not add your own. Safety is of the utmost importance, and by reading the experiment before starting, then following the instructions exactly, you can feel confident that no unexpected results will occur. Ask an adult to help you when you are working with anything sharp or hot. If adult supervision is required, it will be noted in the experiment.

» **RESULTS:** ***An explanation stating exactly what is expected to happen.***

This is an immediate learning tool. If the expected results are achieved, you will know that you did the experiment correctly. If your results are not the same as described in the experiment, carefully read the instructions and start over from the first step.

INTRODUCTION

» **WHY?** ***An explanation of why the results were achieved.***

You will be rewarded with successful experiments if you read each experiment carefully, follow the steps in order, and do not substitute materials.

THE SCIENTIFIC METHOD

Scientists identify a problem or observe an event. Then they seek solutions or explanations through research and experimentation. By doing the experiments in this book, you will learn to follow experimental steps and make observations. You will also learn many scientific principles that have to do with biology.

In the process, the things you see or learn may lead you to new questions. For example, perhaps you have completed the experiment that looks at the movement of water through a leaf. Now you wonder what would happen if you conducted the experiment at different temperatures. That's great! Every scientist is curious and asks new questions about what they learn. When you design a new experiment, it is a good idea to follow the scientific method.

1. Ask a question.
2. Do some research about your question. What do you already know?
3. Come up with a hypothesis, or a possible answer to your question.
4. Design an experiment to test your hypothesis. Make sure the experiment is repeatable.
5. Collect the data and make observations.
6. Analyze your results.
7. Reach a conclusion. Did your results support your hypothesis?

Many times the experiment leads to more questions and a new experiment.

Always remember that when devising your own science experiment, have a knowledgeable adult review it with you before trying it out. Ask them to supervise it as well.

Too Big

Purpose To determine why dinosaur eggs were so small compared to the adult dinosaur.

Materials paper towel

Procedure

1. Hold the paper towel with both hands.
2. Stretch the paper towel slightly and place it against your mouth.
3. Blow through the paper towel. Make a mental note of the effort required to blow through the single layer.
4. Fold the paper towel in half and blow through the two layers. Compare the effort required to blow through the single and double layers.
5. Fold the paper towel in half again.
6. Try to blow through the four layers, and note how much effort it takes to blow through the added layers.

Results It becomes more difficult to blow through the paper towel as the number of layers increases.

Why? The shell of an egg, like the paper towel, permits air to flow through it if the layers are thin. But as the number of layers increases, it is more difficult for the air to pass through. In addition, the liquid inside the egg exerts pressure on the eggshell. Larger eggs require a thicker shell to hold back the increased pressure from the inside. Thicker shells not only would have been very difficult for the baby dinosaur to break out of, but also would have restricted the flow of air through the shell. Thus, the size and thickness of a dinosaur egg, like any egg, is limited.

GRINDERS

PURPOSE To determine how dinosaurs ate their food without grinding teeth.

MATERIALS 20 green leaves from a large tree or bush (ask an adult to select the leaves)
2 resealable plastic bags
5 walnut-sized rocks

PROCEDURE

1. Observe the shape of the leaves and then place 10 leaves in each plastic bag.
2. Add the rocks to one of the bags of leaves.
3. Hold the bag of leaves that does not contain the rocks between the palms of your hands.
4. Rub your hands together vigorously against the plastic bag 25 times. Observe the shape of the leaves.
5. Repeat step 4 with the other bag.

NOTE: Do not rub so hard that you injure your hands.

RESULTS The shape of the leaves in the bag that does not contain the rocks changes slightly or not at all. The leaves in the bag that contained the rocks are crushed.

WHY? Apatosaurus and other dinosaurs with a similar body makeup probably did not chew their food, but swallowed it whole. Paleontologists have found large polished rocks near the rib bones of Apatosaurus fossils. The location of these rocks suggests that they were swallowed, just as modern chickens swallow gravel and use it to grind food inside their bodies. The food inside the dinosaur's body was pulverized by the rocks as the rocks moved around, just as the leaves were ground by the rocks in the bag.

Cooling Off

Purpose To determine how elephants use their ears to cool their bodies.

Materials paper towel
tap water
3-by-5-inch (7.5-by-12.5-cm) index card

Procedure

1. Wet the paper towel with water.
2. Rub the wet towel over the surface of your arm.
3. Hold the index card about 4 inches (10 cm) above your wet arm.
4. Quickly fan the index card back and forth about ten times. Observe any cooling effect on the skin.

Results The fanned wet skin feels cool.

Why? The cooling effect is due to the evaporation of the water from the skin. Evaporation occurs when a liquid absorbs enough heat energy to change from a liquid to a gas. The water takes energy away from the skin when it evaporates, causing the skin to cool. Elephants use their trunks to spray themselves with water; then they fan their bodies with their large ears. The fanning of their ears, like the index card, increases the flow of air across the skin. The moving air speeds the evaporation of the water, thus aiding in the cooling of the skin.

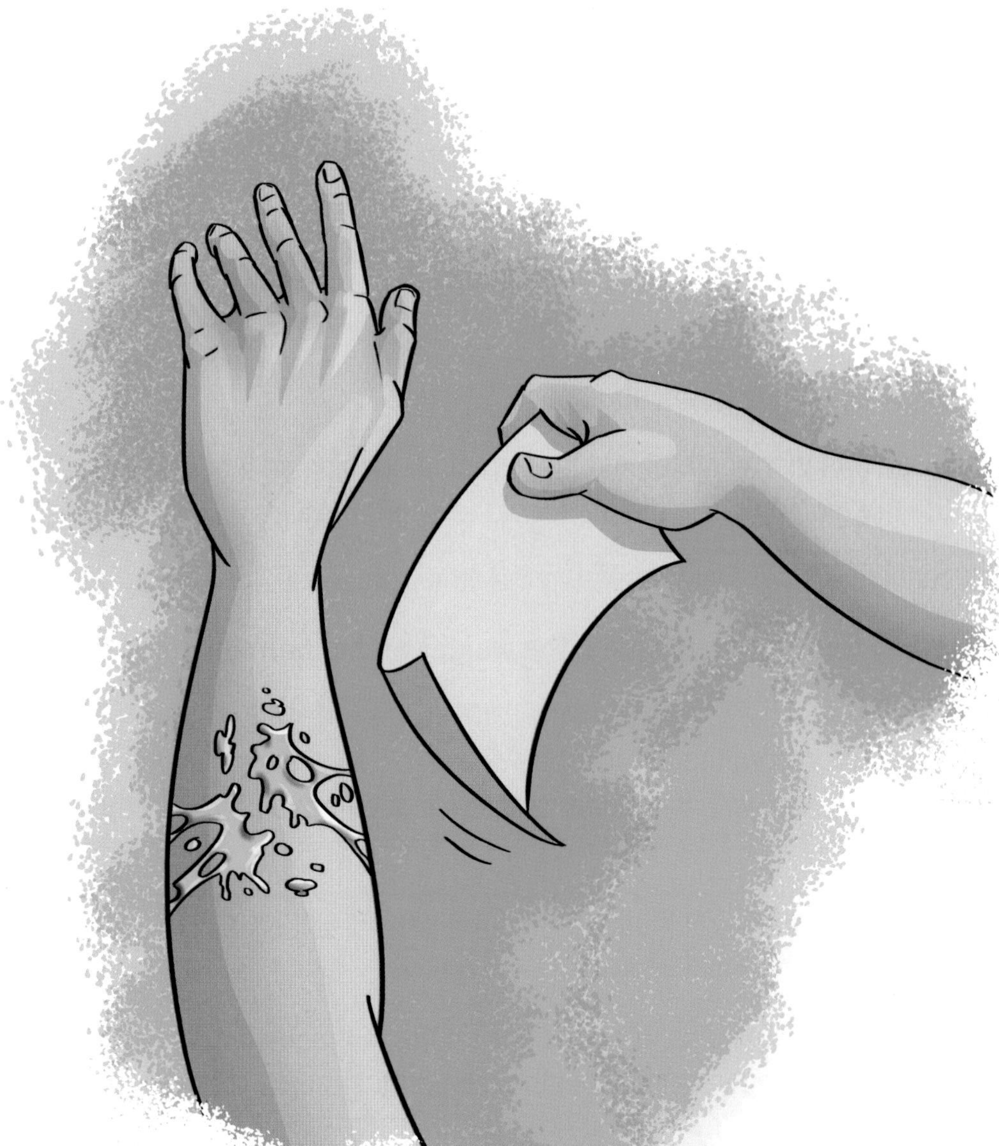

Fatty Insulators

Purpose To determine how the fat layer under the skin keeps an animal warm.

Materials two 7-ounce (210-ml) paper cups
shortening, such as Crisco
2 thermometers
freezer
timer

Procedure

1. Fill one paper cup with shortening.
2. Insert one thermometer into the cup of shortening so that the bulb of the thermometer is in the center of the shortening.
3. Stand the other thermometer in the other paper cup.

NOTE: Lay the cup on its side if the weight of the thermometer tends to topple the cup over.

4. Read and record the temperature shown on each thermometer. Then place the cups with their thermometers in the freezer and shut the door.
5. Read and record the temperature on each thermometer after 15 minutes.

Results In 15 minutes, the readings on the thermometer placed in the shortening changed very little, but the temperature inside the empty cup decreased rapidly.

WHY? The shortening, like the fat layer under the skin of animals, acts as an insulator and, thus, restricts the heat flow away from the warm inner body to the frigid air outside the body. The heat inside the shortening, like that in an animal's body, is lost, but, because of the insulating fat, the loss is very slow. Food eaten by animals provides energy that continuously replaces the lost heat.

FEATHER FEATURES

PURPOSE To study parts of a feather.

MATERIALS feather
magnifying lens

NOTE: Purchase the feather at a craft store. Do not use a feather found on the ground.

PROCEDURE

1. Gently pull apart one part of the feather as shown.
2. Study the surface of the feather with the lens and note the edges where the feather is pulled apart.

RESULTS There are parallel ridges coming off both sides of the hard tubelike center of the feather. Where the feather is separated, there are hairlike structures along both separated edges.

WHY? The feather is made up of a tubelike center called the shaft; the rest of the feather is called the vane. The vane is made up of barbs that look like strings coming off the shaft in parallel rows. Where two barbs are separated, tiny barbules grow from each of the barbs. On one side of a barb, the barbules are more hooked.

Barbules
Break
Barbs
Vane
Shaft

ZIP

PURPOSE To demonstrate how birds repair their feathers.

MATERIALS resealable plastic bag
feather

NOTE: Purchase the feather at a craft store. Do not use a feather found on the ground.

PROCEDURE

1. Open the bag.
2. Put the open edges of the bag together and use your fingers to "zip" the bag closed.
3. Separate the vane on one side of the feather's shaft.
4. Use your fingers to push the separated section of the vane back together.
5. Move your fingers across the top and bottom of the feather in the same manner you "zipped" the plastic bag closed.

RESULTS The bag and the feather both can be closed.

WHY? Both the bag and the feather have edges that fit together. The vane of the feather is made of barbs with a rolled edge on one side and tiny hooks on the other side. These edges interlock when pressed together, just as the edges of the bag interlock. Birds press the barbs together with their beaks to keep their feathers smooth.

Sipper

Purpose To determine why hummingbirds have long, slender bills.

Materials tall, slender vase
tap water
drinking straw

Procedure

1. Fill the vase half full with water. Lower the straw into the vase.
2. With your finger over the end of the straw, lift the straw so that its open end is above the water.
3. Lift your finger from the straw's opening.

Results Water pours out of the straw into the vase.

Why? The straw is long enough to reach and remove the water in the vase. Hummingbirds have long, slender, hollow bills like the straw. The long, slender shape of their bills makes it easier for them to probe flowers for nectar.

Night Crawlers

Purpose To determine how earthworms respond to light.

Materials scissors
shoe box with lid
flashlight
tape
notebook paper
tap water
paper towels
10 earthworms (purchase at a bait shop or dig your own)
timer

Procedure

1. Cut a hole slightly smaller than the flashlight's end near the edge of the shoebox lid.
2. Tape a sheet of notebook paper to the lid so that it hangs about 1 Inch (2.5 cm) from the floor of the shoe box, and about 4 inches (10 cm) from the edge opposite the hole in the lid.
3. Place moistened paper towels in the bottom of the box.
4. Place the earthworms in the box under where the hole in the lid is.
5. Position the flashlight over the hole and turn it on.
6. Leave the box undisturbed for 30 minutes, then open the lid and observe the position of the worms.
7. Return the worms to their natural surroundings—soil in a shady

area outside.

RESULTS The worms crawl away from the white light and under the paper partition where it is darker.

WHY? Earthworms have no obvious sense organs such as eyes, but the worms respond to white light. Earthworms often surface at night and, therefore, are referred to as night crawlers.

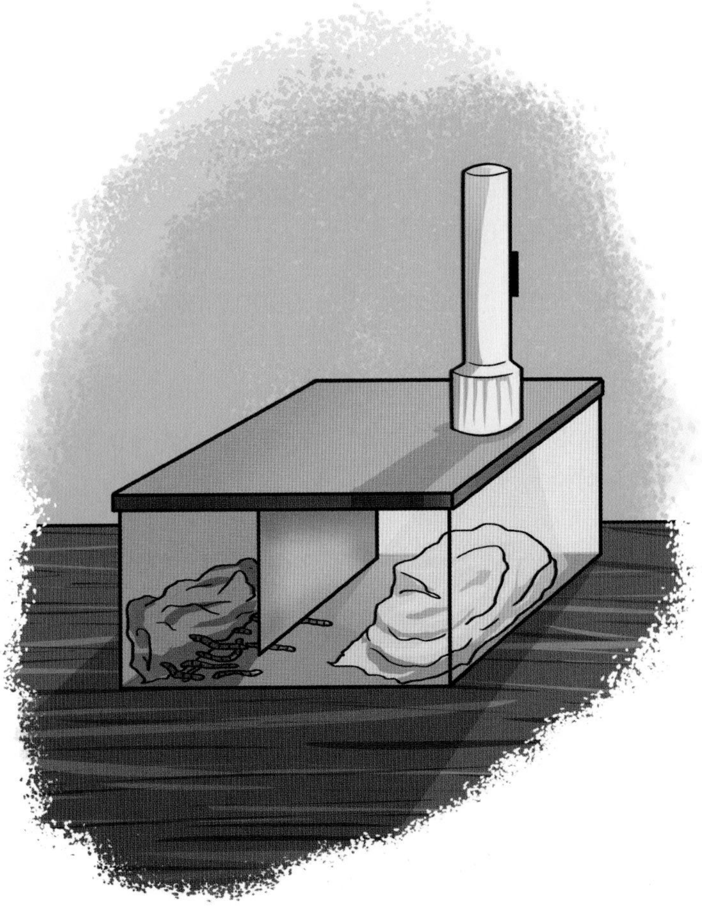

Earthworm Farm

Purpose To produce an environment suitable for earthworms.

Materials 2 cups (500 ml) soil
quart (liter) jar
tap water
1 cup (250 ml) peat moss
earthworms (purchase at a bait shop or dig your own)
apple peelings
dark construction paper
rubber band

Procedure

1. Pour the soil into the jar. Moisten the soil with water and keep it moist throughout the experiment.
2. Add the peat moss. Then put the worms into the jar.
3. Add the apple peelings.
4. Wrap the paper around the jar and secure with a rubber band. Place the jar in a shady, cool place.
5. Remove the paper and observe the jar every day for 7 days.
6. Return the worms to their natural surroundings—soil in a shady area outside.

Results The worms start wiggling and burrow into the soil. Tunnels are seen in the soil after a few days. The apple peelings disappear and pellets appear on the surface of the soil.

WHY? An earthworm does not have jaws or teeth, but a muscle draws soil particles into its mouth. The worm extracts food from the soil, and the remaining part of the soil passes through the worm's body unchanged. Waste pellets called casts contain undigested soil and are deposited by the worm on the surface of the soil.

CHIRPER

PURPOSE To determine how temperature affects a cricket's chirp.

MATERIALS cricket (purchase at a bait shop, pet store, or catch your own)
quart (liter) jar
old nylon stocking
rubber band
stopwatch

PROCEDURE

NOTE: This activity should be performed on a warm day. Begin the activity in the early morning.

1. Place the cricket in the jar. Stretch the stocking over the mouth of the jar and secure it with the rubber band.
2. In the morning, the cooler part of the day, place the jar outside in the shade, then wait about 20 minutes.
3. Use the stopwatch to time yourself and count how many times the crickets chirps in 15 seconds. Count the chirps again in another 15-second period.
4. Repeat steps 2 and 3 during the hottest part of the day.
5. Release the cricket outside. Results The cricket chirps more during the hottest part of the day.

WHY? The temperature affects the activity of many animals. They are generally more sluggish when they are cool and more active when they are warm. Crickets are more active and chirp more when they are warm.

DISTINCTIVE

PURPOSE To determine how butterflies and moths differ.

MATERIALS insect net
butterfly and moth (instructions for catching below)
2 large jars
2 old nylon knee-high stockings
2 rubber bands

PROCEDURE

1. Use the insect net to catch a butterfly and a moth for this study.
2. Place the captured insects in separate jars. You can remove them from the net by holding the net over the jar and gently shaking out the insect.
3. Stretch a stocking over the mouth of each jar and secure with a rubber band.
4. View both insects through the glass and compare their differences.
5. Release the insects outside.

RESULTS The insects differ in the shape of their antennae and abdomen and how they hold their wings.

WHY? The butterfly holds its wings upward when resting, and the moth rests with its wings spread out. The butterfly's antennae are slender and clubbed at the end. Moths have all shapes and sizes of antennae, but their antennae are never clubbed and many are feathery. The body and abdomen of the moth is thicker and larger than the butterfly's.

GRASSHOPPER

PURPOSE To determine the number of body parts of a grasshopper.

MATERIALS insect net
grasshopper (instructions for catching below)
plastic vegetable bag
magnifying lens

PROCEDURE

1. It's better to use a dead grasshopper for this study, but if a dead grasshopper is not found, catch a live one with the net and place it in the plastic bag.
2. Move the live grasshopper to the corner of the bag so that it cannot move around.
3. Use the magnifying lens to study the body of the insect.
4. Release the live grasshopper outside.

RESULTS The grasshopper's body has three main parts.

WHY? Grasshoppers, like all insects, have three main body parts: the head, thorax, and abdomen.

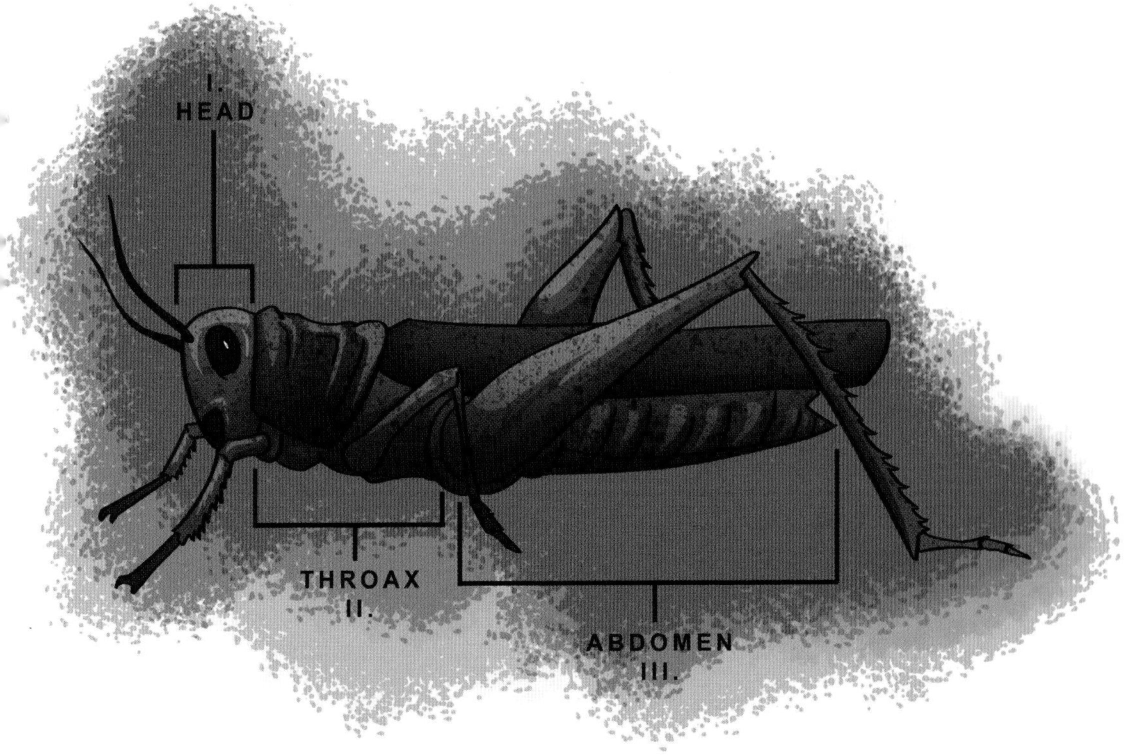
I.
HEAD
THROAX
II.
ABDOMEN
III.

BZZZZZ

PURPOSE To determine why insects make buzzing sounds.

MATERIALS rubber band (large enough to fit tightly around the glass)
juice glass
index card

PROCEDURE

1. Stretch the rubber band vertically around the glass, as shown in the diagram.
2. Pluck the rubber band with your finger.
3. Immediately touch the rubber band with a corner of the card.

RESULTS A buzzing sound is heard.

WHY? Sound is produced when objects vibrate (move quickly back and forth). The pitch is the property of sound that makes it high or low. A high-pitched sound, such as the buzzing of the paper, is produced when an object vibrates many times per second. The same highpitched buzzing sound is produced by the rapid back-and- forth movement of an insect's wings.

HIDDEN

PURPOSE To demonstrate how color helps to protect an animal.

MATERIALS scissors
ruler
2 sheets of construction paper (1 black and 1 orange)
2 sheets of newspaper (use sheets with print only—no pictures)
pencil
helper

PROCEDURE

1. Cut two 3-by-5-inch (7.5-by-12.5-cm) rectangles from each sheet of construction paper and from one sheet of newspaper.
2. Stack the rectangles together. Draw the largest fish possible on the top piece.
3. Cut out the fish, making sure to cut through all 6 layers of paper. Do not allow your helper to see the fish before the experiment starts.
4. Lay the uncut sheet of newspaper on the floor at the feet of your helper.
5. Ask your helper to close his or her eyes while you scatter the paper fish on the newspaper. Be sure to lay the newspaper fish with the print-only side facing up.
6. When you say "Go" have your helper open his or her eyes, quickly look at the newspaper, count the paper fish that are laying on the

newspaper, and then immediately raise his or her eyes from the newspaper.

RESULTS Usually people see only the black and orange fish.

WHY? The newspaper fish are an example of camouflage. Camouflage occurs when an animal's color blends into the color of its environment (the natural surroundings of an organism). Camouflage makes it difficult for an animal to be seen by a predator (an animal that lives by killing and eating other animals).

DECOMPOSERS

PURPOSE To observe the effects of yeast on food decomposition.

MATERIALS butter knife
banana
2 resealable plastic bags
measuring spoon
dry yeast
marking pen

PROCEDURE

1. Cut 2 slices from the banana.
2. Place one slice of banana inside each plastic bag.
3. Sprinkle 1½ teaspoon (2.5 ml) of yeast on one of the banana slices.
4. Close both bags.
5. Label the bag containing the yeast Y.
6. Check each bag daily for one week. Observe and compare the amount and rate of decomposition of both slices.

RESULTS The banana covered with yeast shows the most and fastest decomposition.

WHY? Yeast is one of about 100,000 different kinds of organisms that make up the fungi group. Fungi must depend on other organisms for food. The yeast feeds on the banana, causing the banana to break into smaller parts. This breakdown is referred to as decomposition. Decomposers, like yeast, are an important part of our world because there is much dead material that must be broken into smaller parts and reused by plants and animals. The fertilizer used on plants and gardens has many decomposers working in it to make the material usable by the plants.

Fuzz Balls

Purpose To create an environment in which to grow penicillium.

Materials 2 oranges
2 cotton balls
2 lemons
tap water
bowl
2 plastic bread sacks with twist ties

Procedure

1. Place the fruit in the bowl and expose it to the air for one day.
2. In each bread sack, place an orange, a lemon, and a cotton ball moistened with water.
3. Secure the ends of the sacks with a twist tie.
4. Place one sack in the refrigerator and the other in a warm, dark place.
5. Leave the sacks closed for two weeks and observe the fruit through the sacks as often as possible.
6. Discard the unopened bags.

Results The fruit in the refrigerator has little or no change, but the other fruit has turned into blue-green fuzzy balls.

Why? The green powdery growth on the outside of the fruit is penicillium. Penlclllllum is a mold from which penicillin, a medicine that kills germs, is made. Penicillium, like most molds, grows faster and in more abundance in moist warm places. This is why foods become more moldy in the summertime. Bread at room temperature molds more quickly than bread placed in a refrigerator. Cooling foods slows down the growth of mold, and freezing keeps foods fresh for much longer periods of time.

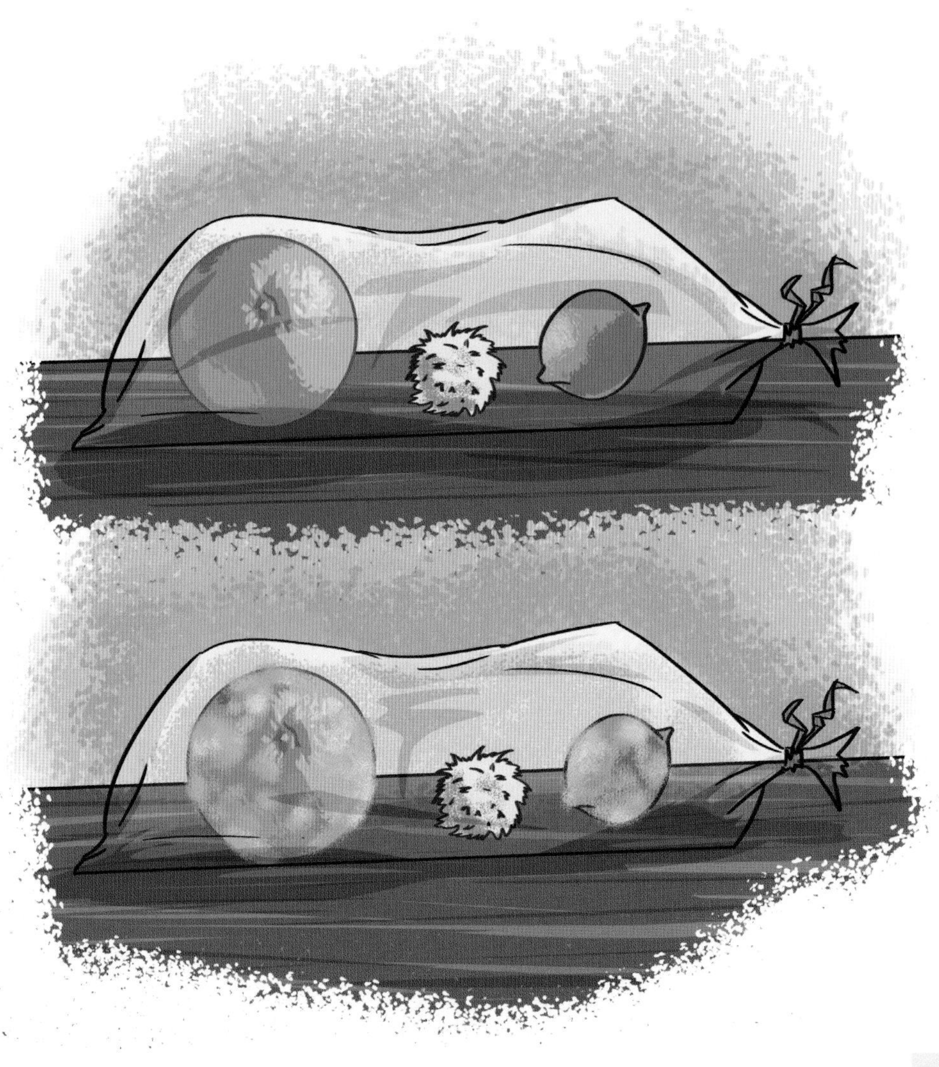

Mini-Organisms

Purpose To test the effect of preservatives on bacterial growth.

Materials chicken bouillon cube
1 cup (250 ml) warm tap water
3 small clear drinking glasses
1 teaspoon (5 ml) table salt
marking pen
masking tape
1 teaspoon (5 ml} white vinegar

Procedure

1. Dissolve the bouillon cube in the warm water.
2. Divide the solution equally between the 3 glasses.
3. Add the salt to one of the glasses. Use the marking pen and tape to label the glass Salt.
4. Add the vinegar to the second glass and label it Vinegar.
5. Label the third glass Control because it will not contain a preservative.
6. Place the three glasses in a warm place and observe after two days. Discard the contents of each glass.

Results The solution containing vinegar is the clearest. The control is the most cloudy.

Why? The cloudiness is due to the presence of large quantities of bacteria. The glasses containing the preservatives salt and vinegar are clearer than the control because the preservatives inhibit, or slow down, the growth of bacteria. Vinegar inhibits the bacterial growth better than salt does.

Passing Through

Purpose To symbolize how size affects movement of particles through a cell membrane.

Materials ½ cup (125 ml) table salt
1½ cup (125 ml) dry pinto beans
quart (liter) jar, with lid
colander
large bowl
helper

Procedure

1. Pour the salt and beans into the jar.
2. Secure the lid and shake the jar back and forth several times to thoroughly mix the salt and beans.
3. Hold the colander over the bowl as your helper opens the jar and pours its contents into the colander.
4. Gently shake the colander up and down several times.
5. Observe the contents of the colander and bowl.

Results The salt falls through the holes in the colander and into the bowl. The beans remain in the colander.

Why? Cell membranes act like the colander, allowing passage of only those particles small enough to pass through the holes (in this case, salt). Particles larger than the holes (pinto beans) are prevented from passing through. Cells have a semipermeable membrane, which allows some materials to pass through but not others. Size is one selecting factor. Water passes through, but large particles do not.

Limp Spuds

Purpose To demonstrate osmosis.

Materials 1 tablespoon (15 ml) table salt
1 cup (230 ml) tap water
small bowl
spoon
potato
timer
adult helper

Procedure

1. Add the salt and water to the bowl. Stir.
2. Have an adult cut 3 potato slices, about 114 inch (6 mm) thick.
3. Place the potato slices in the bowl of salt water.
4. After 15 minutes, pick up the potato slices one at atime. Test their hardness by trying to bend the slices.

Results The slices are very limp and bend easily.

Why? Osmosis is the movement of water through a semipermeable membrane. Water always moves through a membrane toward the side containing the most dissolved material, such as salt. The potato slices soaked in salt water feel limp because they have lost some of the original water inside their cells. The water from inside each potato slice moves out of the potato through cell membranes and into the bowl of salt water.

SALT

TRANSPORTER

PURPOSE To observe the movement of water through a leaf.

MATERIALS juice glass
tap water
red food coloring
scissors
large tree leaf, such as oak
adult helper

PROCEDURE

1. Fill the glass about one-fourth full with water.
2. Add enough food coloring to make the water a deep red color.
3. Ask an adult to cut off the end of the leaf's stem.
4. Stand the leaf in the glass of colored water
5. Observe the color of the leaf for 2 days.

RESULTS The red color slowly moves through the leaf, first following the pattern of the leaf veins and then spreading throughout the leaf.

WHY? The plant leaf and stem contain tubes called xylem. These tubes transport water from the roots to other parts of the plant. In this activity, the colored water from the glass moves through these tubes to all parts of the leaf.

SWEETENED LEAVES

PURPOSE To demonstrate how nutrients in the soil are transported to the leaves of plants.

MATERIALS masking tape
marking pen
3 glasses
2 tablespoons (30 ml) sugar
tap water
spoon
3 fresh stalks of celery with leaves

PROCEDURE

NOTE: Never taste anything in a laboratory setting unless you are sure that it does not contain harmful chemicals or materials.

1. Use the tape and marking pen to label the glasses 1 , 2, and 3, respectively.
2. Add 1 tablespoon (15 ml) of sugar to glasses 2 and 3.
3. Fill glasses 1 and 2 half full with water. Stir the water in glass 2 to dissolve the sugar.
4. Stand a stalk of celery in each glass.
5. Place the glasses in a refrigerator.
6. Wait 48 hours, then taste the leaves from each celery stalk.

RESULTS The leaves on the celery standing in glass 2 taste sweet and those of the celery in the other glasses do not.

WHY? As it dissolves sugar, water dissolves nutrients in soil and moves into the plant through the roots. From the roots, this liquid moves through xylem tubes to the leaves and other parts of the plant.

TRICKERY

PURPOSE To make a spring plant flower in the winter.

MATERIALS 4 round toothpicks
flower bulb, such as hyacinth or paper whites
quart (liter) jar
tap water
sheet of dark construction paper
transparent tape
adult helper

PROCEDURE

NOTE: This activity should be performed in the winter.

1. Ask an adult to insert toothpicks horizontally into the bulb on all four sides.
2. Fill the jar nearly full with water.
3. Wrap the paper around the jar and secure with tape.
4. Place the bulb in the jar so that the toothpicks rest on the mouth of the jar and the bottom of the bulb just touches the top of the water. Remove some of the water if it rises above the bottom of the bulb.
5. Place the bulb and jar in a warm, lighted area, such as near a window, for 2 to 4 weeks.

RESULTS The bulb develops roots, stems, and a flower.

WHY? Bulbs normally sprout in the spring when the soil becomes warm.

Plants do not think and cannot really be tricked, but when you put the bulb in a warm place, the bulb behaves as if it were spring and starts to grow. The dark paper protects the roots from light like the soil does when plants are grown in the ground.

Helicopter Seeds

Purpose To demonstrate the movement of fallen maple seeds.

Materials
- pencil
- ruler
- sheet of typing paper
- scissors
- small paper clip

Procedure

1. Draw a triangle with 4-inch (10-cm) sides on the paper.
2. Cut a 1-inch (2.5-cm) slit in the center of one side, perpendicular to the side.
3. Draw a fold line at the end of the slit, perpendicular to the slit and parallel to the side in which you cut the slit.
4. Label the area left of the slit with an A, label the area right of the slit with a B, and write Body on the lower part, as shown in the diagram.
5. Fold along the fold line so that area A points away from you and area B points toward you.
6. Place the paper clip across the pointed tip of the paper.
7. Hold the paper as high as possible and drop it.

Results The paper twirls around.

Why? The paper is shaped so that as it drops, it twirls like the blades of a helicopter. Maple seeds have a similar shape and also twirl as they fall. Both the paper and the maple seeds twirl because some of the air hitting the undersides of the blades is directed toward the body. Since the blades are on different sides, this air flow pushes the body from different directions, causing it to spin around.

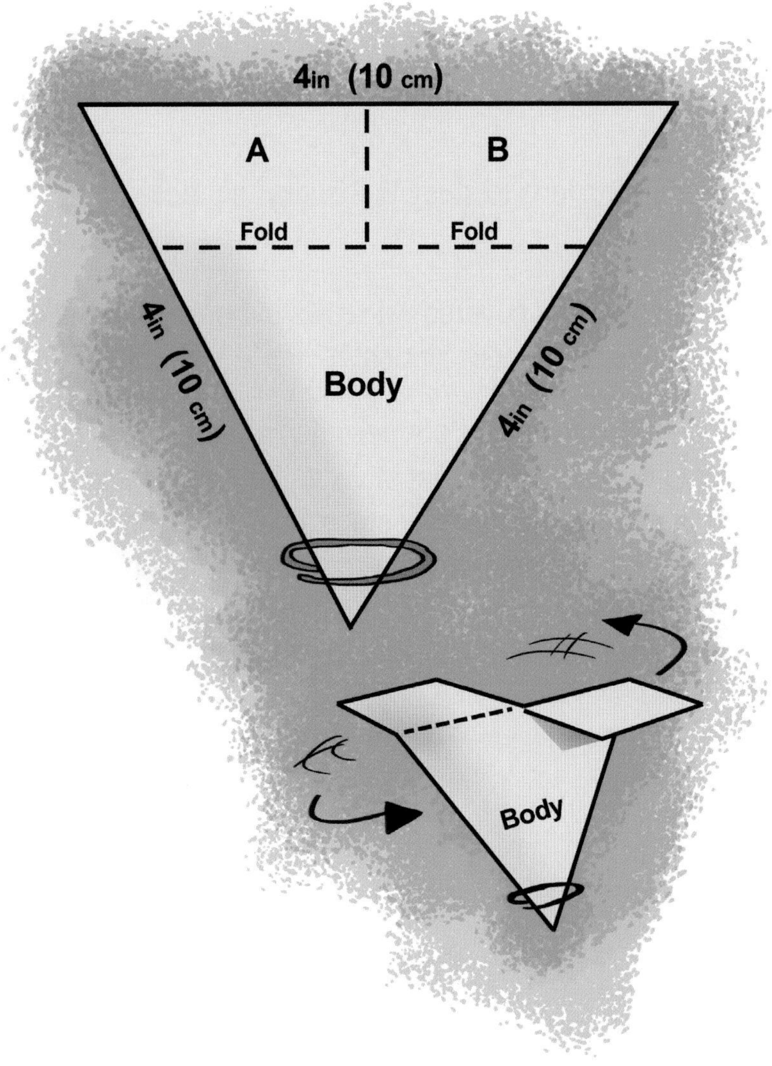

STUCK

PURPOSE To determine how cocklebur seeds and hook-and-loop fasteners like Velcro are alike.

MATERIALS 1-by-6-inch (2.5-by-15-cm) pair of hook-and-loop fastener strips (purchase at a fabric store)
magnifying lens

PROCEDURE

1. Use the magnifying lens to study the "sticky" surfaces of the hook-and-loop strips.

RESULTS One surface is covered with rows of hooks, and the other is covered with a mass of threadlike loops.

WHY? Hook-and-loop fasteners are designed after the cocklebur seed, which is covered with hooks that get stuck in the fur of animals when they brush against the seed. The fastener strips' hooks and loops are usually made from a blend of polyester and nylon. Like cocklebur seeds, the hooks on the surface of one fastener strip catch in the loops on the surface of the other strip. The joined hooks and loops hold the strips tightly together.

GLOSSARY

BARBS The separate stringlike structures of a feather's vane.

BARBULES Growths on each side of a feather's barb.

CAMOUFLAGE When the color of an organism blends into that of its environment, making the organism difficult to find.

CASTS Waste pellets from earthworms containing undigested soil.

DECOMPOSITION The process of breaking down; decay.

ENVIRONMENT The natural surroundings of an organism.

EVAPORATION To change from a liquid to a gas.

FUNGI A group of organisms that lack chlorophyll and must depend on other organisms for food.

INSULATOR A material that helps prevent temperature changes by slowing the transfer of heat.

OSMOSIS The movement of water through a semipermeable membrane; movement is toward the side with the least water concentration.

PENICILLIUM A mold from which penicillin, a medicine that kills germs, is made.

PREDATOR An animal that lives by killing and eating other animals.

SEMIPERMEABLE MEMBRANE A membrane that allows some, but not all, materials to pass through.

SHAFT The tubelike center of a feather.

VANE The part of a feather excluding the shaft.

VIBRATE To move quickly back and forth.

XYLEM Tiny tubes in the stalk of a plant and leaf stem, which transport water and food to the plant's cells.

For More Information

The National Geographic Society
1145 17th Street, NW
Washington, DC 20036
Museum (202) 857-7700
website: http://www.nationalgeographic.com/
The National Geographic Society has been inspiring people to care about the planet since 1888. It is one of the largest nonprofit scientific and educational institutions in the world. Read their Kids magazine, enter the National Geographic Bee, or visit the museum.

National Science Foundation (NSF)
4201 Wilson Boulevard
Arlington, Virginia 22230, USA
(703) 292-5111
website: http://www.nsf.gov/
The NSF is dedicated to science, engineering, and education. Learn how to be a Citizen Scientist, read about the latest scientific discoveries, and discover the newest innovations in technology.

Royal Botanical Gardens
680 Plains Road West
Burlington, ON
Canada
(800) 694-4769
website: http://www.rbg.ca/
The Royal Botanical Gardens is the largest botanical garden in Canada, a National Historic Site, and a registered charitable organization with a goal of bringing together people, plants, and nature.

The National Zoological Park
3001 Connecticut Avenue NW
Washington, D.C. 20008
(202) 633-4888
website: https://nationalzoo.si.edu/
The National Zoological Park is a part of the Smithsonian Institution, the world's largest museum and research complex. Join a Nature Camp, watch the newest arrivals at the zoo through the Live Animal Cam, or learn more about wildlife research expeditions.

The Society for Science and the Public
Student Science
1719 N Street, NW
Washington, D.C. 20036
(800) 552-4412
website: https://student.societyforscience.org/
The Society for Science and the Public presents many science project resources, such as science news for students, the latest updates on the Intel Science Talent Search and the Intel International Science and Engineering Fair, and information about cool jobs and doing science.

WEBSITES

Because of the changing nature of Internet links, Rosen Publishing has developed an online list of websites related to the subject of this book. This site is updated regularly. Please use this link to access this list:

http://www.rosenlinks.com/JVCW/bio

For Further Reading

Ardley, Neil. *101 Great Science Experiments*. New York: DK Ltd., 2014.

Buczynski, Sandy. *Designing a Winning Science Fair Project* (Information Explorer Junior). Ann Arbor, MI: Cherry Lake Publishing, 2014.

Franchino, Vicky. *Animal Camouflage* (True Book). New York: Children's Press, 2016.

Goldish, Meish. *Inside the Worm's Hole* (Snug As a Bug: Where Bugs Live). New York: Bearport Publishing, 2014.

Gray, Leon. *Amazing Animal Engineers* (Fact Finders: Animal Scientists). North Mankato, MN: Capstone Press, 2016.

Hawkins, Jay. *It's Alive! The Science of Plants and Living Things* (Big Bang Science Experiments). New York: Windmill Books, 2013.

Henneberg, Susan. *Creating Science Fair Projects with Cool New Digital Tools* (Way Beyond PowerPoint: Making 21st Century Presentations). New York: Rosen Central, 2014.

Latham, Donna. *Backyard Biology: Investigate Habitats Outside Your Door with 25 Projects* (Build It Yourself). White River Junction, VT: Nomad Press, 2013.

Lawrence, Ellen. *Dirt* (Fundamental Experiments). New York: Bearport Publishing, 2013.

Lawrence, Ellen. *Why Do Most Plants Need Soil?* (Down & Dirty: The Secrets of Soil). New York: Bearport Publishing, 2016.

Margles, Samantha. *Mythbusters Science Fair Book*. New York: Scholastic,

2011.

Marsico, Katie. *Step-by-Step Experiments with Life Cycles* (Step-by-Step Experiments). Mankato, MN: The Child's World, 2012.

INDEX